The Cats Gallery of Western Art

Susan Herbert.

SUSAN HERBERT

The Cats Gallery of Western Art

With 63 colour plates

Thames & Hudson

Frontispiece:

Cover of the Coffin of Tutankhamun
c. 1340 BC

The illustrations in this book were first published in two separate volumes,
The Cats Gallery of Art and *The Cats History of Western Art*.
This combined volume first published in the United Kingdom in 2002 by
Thames & Hudson Ltd, 181A High Holborn, London WC1V 7QX

British Library Cataloguing in Publication Data
A catalogue record for this book is available from the British Library
ISBN 0-500-28349-4

Printed and bound in Singapore

Foreword

PROFESSOR MARMALADE KATZENBOGE

I have no way of knowing whether Susan Herbert is aware of the paper I published in 1949 (in the learned *Rundschau der Kunstgeschichte*) on the subject of the substitution of cats for the models in well-known art works, but the pages that follow indicate at least an extraordinary sympathy of outlook. For Miss Herbert has unwittingly, or perhaps even wittingly, who knows? demonstrated in a definitive way that my thesis, presented over fifty years ago to the Faculty of Göttingen University, was not merely an example of academic fireworks – a form of twisting the lion's tail, as they aptly express it in Anglo-American circles – but a true and accurate hypothesis based on sound art-historical principles.

*W*hat I suggested in my by now famous treatise was that many of our Western masterpieces and favoured paintings might be viewed afresh if only they were repainted with cats instead of people. I held it for probable that if, for instance, the Mona Lisa were a furry feline rather than a smug human female, we would come much closer to Leonardo's primal impulses in undertaking that picture. And here, on page 25, is the proof!

*I*n an elaborate painting such a Botticelli's *Birth of Venus*, with its wealth of platonic undertones and hints of Renaissance allegory, surely the sheer beauty of the Goddess of Love as she emerges from the foam of the sea is a distraction from the philosophical scheme of the great work and its subtle allusions to Greek mythology. One look at page 20 will show how useful it is to overcome that distraction

*O*ne does not have to be a rabid ailourophile to appreciate this gallery of art works devoted to the independent, aloof, four-legged creatures who tolerate the company of human beings with barely concealed contempt. And yet, how charming they can be – as milkmaids, as aristocratic ladies, as kings and queens and cavaliers. . . Personally, I have always been partial to whiskers and fluffy tails, and a cat's purring is for me as sweet a form of music as Schubert's *Lieder*.

*B*ut I wander from the point. . . I recommend to you the pioneering work of Susan Herbert in presenting a gallery of famous and much-loved art works with a piquant difference. She has, as it happens, done me a professional service, but she merits a miaow of thanks from the general public too.

POT BY EXEKIAS

(*c.* 550 to 525 BC)

Achilles Slaying Penthesilea

❧

ROMAN
FRESCO
Venus Chastising Cupid

❧

SIXTH-
CENTURY
MOSAIC,
CHURCH OF
SAN VITALE,
RAVENNA

Empress Theodora

❧

THE LIMBURG BROTHERS

c. 1415

'April'
from *Les Très
Riches Heures
du Duc
de Berry*

❧

JAN VAN EYCK

c. 1390 -1441

The Arnolfini Marriage

❧

JAN VAN EYCK
c. 1390-1441

*Portrait
of the Artist's
Wife*

❧

GIOVANNI
BELLINI
c. 1430-1516

*Doge Leonardo
Loredan*

ਤਰ

SANDRO
BOTTICELLI
c. 1444-1510

The Birth of Venus

❧

SANDRO
BOTTICELLI
c. 1444-1510
Primavera

LEONARDO
DA VINCI

1452–1519

Mona Lisa

❧

LEONARDO
DA VINCI

1452–1519

*Lady
with an
Ermine*

TITIAN

1476/77
or 1489/90-1576

Portrait of
a Young Man

MICHELANGELO BUONARROTI

1475-1564

The Creation of Adam

(detail from the Sistine Chapel)

~&~

RAPHAEL
1483-1520

Pope Leo X

❧

HANS HOLBEIN
THE YOUNGER
1497-1543

*Portrait
of Henry VIII*

PIETER
BRUEGHEL
THE ELDER
c. 1520–1569

The Peasant
Dance

PETER PAUL
RUBENS

1577-1640

Rubens and
Isabella Brandt
under a
Honeysuckle
Bower

❧

MARCUS
GHEERAERTS
THE YOUNGER
1561/62-1635

Portrait of
Queen Elizabeth I

❦

FRANS HALS

c. 1580-1666

The Laughing Cavalier

❧

ANTHONY VAN DYCK

1599-1641

King Charles I
(Triple Portrait)

❧

DIEGO DE SILVA Y VELAZQUEZ

1599-1660

Las Meninas

❧

DIEGO DE SILVA Y VELAZQUEZ

1599-1660

The Rokeby Venus

REMBRANDT
HARMENSZ VAN RIJN
1606-1669

The Night Watch

REMBRANDT
HARMENSZ VAN RIJN
1606-1669

*The Syndics
of the
Clothmakers'
Guild*

JAN VERMEER
OF DELFT
1632-1675

The Milkmaid

❧

JAN VERMEER
OF DELFT

1632-1675

The Artist
in His Studio

❧

JEAN-ANTOINE
WATTEAU
1684-1721

*Les Fêtes
vénitiennes*

❧

WILLIAM HOGARTH
1697-1764

The Brothel Scene from *The Rake's Progress*

❧

FRANÇOIS
BOUCHER
1703-1770

Madame
de Pompadour

❧

SIR JOSHUA
REYNOLDS

1723-1792

*Lady
Elizabeth Delmé
and Her
Children*

THOMAS
GAINSBOROUGH

1727-1788

Blue Boy

THOMAS
GAINSBOROUGH
1727-1788

Portrait of
Mary Graham

❧

FRANCISCO
JOSÉ DE GOYA
Y LUCIENTES

1746-1828

The Clothed Maja

FRANCISCO
JOSÉ DE GOYA
Y LUCIENTES

1746-1828

The Family
of Charles IV

JACQUES-LOUIS DAVID

1748-1825

The Death of Marat

WILLIAM BLAKE

1757-1827

The Ancient
of Days

❦

JEAN-AUGUSTE-DOMINIQUE INGRES
1780-1867

Madame
Moitessier

❧

EUGÈNE
DELACROIX
1791-1863

Study for
*Greece Expiring
in the Ruins
of Missalonghi*

❧

GUSTAVE
COURBET
1819-1877

The Meeting

FORD
MADOX BROWN

1821-1893

The Last of England

❦

DANTE GABRIEL ROSSETTI
1828-1882

Proserpine

❧

SIR JOHN EVERETT MILLAIS

1829-1896

Ophelia

❧

SIR JOHN EVERETT MILLAIS
1829-1896
My First Sermon

SIR JOHN EVERETT MILLAIS

1829-1896

My Second Sermon

SIR JOHN
EVERETT MILLAIS
1829-1896
Bubbles

❧

HENRY WALLIS

1830-1916

The Death
of Chatterton

ÉDOUARD
MANET
1832-1883
The Balcony

❧

ÉDOUARD
MANET
1832-1883

*The Bar
at the
Folies-Bergère*

ÉDOUARD
MANET

1832–1883

Argenteuil

ARTHUR HUGHES
1832-1915
April Love

EDGAR DEGAS
1834-1917
Dancing Class

❦

JAMES MCNEILL WHISTLER

1834-1903

Arrangement in Black and Grey (Portrait of the Artist's Mother)

❧

JAMES TISSOT

1836-1903

Colonel Burnaby

❧

JAMES TISSOT
1836-1903
The Fan

❧

CLAUDE MONET

1840-1926

Women
in the Garden

AUGUSTE RENOIR
1841-1919
The Loge

HENRI ROUSSEAU

1844-1910

Self-Portrait

❧

Susan Herbert

JOHN WILLIAM
WATERHOUSE
1849-1917

The Lady of Shalott

❧

VINCENT
VAN GOGH
1853-1890

Self-Portrait

❧

VINCENT
VAN GOGH
1853-1890

Doctor Gachet

❧

GEORGES
SEURAT
1859–1891

Bathers,
Asnières

❧

FRANÇOIS FLAMENG
1856-1923

Portrait of
Princess
Z.N.Yusupova

❧